G000059749

A gift for:

Linda
_____

From:

Nana with love xxx
_____

Happy Birthday

13. 7. 03.

*Hold onto
a true friend
with both hands.*

NIGERIAN PROVERB

God's Promises® for You,
F·R·I·E·N·D

Illustrated by Gwen Babbitt

Copyright of text © 2003 by the J. Countryman division of Thomas Nelson Inc.,
Nashville, Tennessee 37214

Copyright of illustrations © 2003 by Gwen Babbitt

Project Manager—Terri Gibbs

All rights reserved. No portion of this publication may be reproduced, stored
in a retrieval system or transmitted in any form by any means—electronic,
mechanical, photocopying, recording, or any other—except for brief quotations
in printed reviews, without the prior written permission of the publisher.

All Scripture quotations in this book, unless otherwise indicated,
are from the New King James Version (NKJV) ©1979, 1980, 1982, 1992,
Thomas Nelson, Inc., Publisher, and are used by permission.
www.thomasnelson.com
www.jcountryman.com

Designed by Left Coast Design, Portland, Oregon.

ISBN: 08499-9648-1

Printed and bound in Italy

A smile is the shortest distance between friends.

ANONYMOUS

Blessed are the merciful
For they shall obtain mercy.
MATTHEW 5:7

*Blessed are they
who have the gift
of making friends
for it is one of
God's best gifts.*

THOMAS HUGHES

He will love you and bless
you and multiply you.

DEUTERONOMY 7:13

God's love is a sun
that never sets.
It is always, always,
at its full noonday glory.

ARTHUR JOHN GOSSIP

Wait on the LORD; be of good courage,
and He shall strengthen your heart.

PSALM 27:14

The soul that waits upon
the Lord is the soul that is
entirely surrendered to Him.

HANNAH WHITALL SMITH

The humble also shall increase
their joy in the LORD.

ISAIAH 29:19

Knowing that we are
hopelessly weak is the first step
toward receiving God's gift
of might and strength.

MARVA J. DAWN

A friend loves at all times.

PROVERBS 17:17

*A friend is someone
to whom I do not have
to explain myself.*

INGRID TROBISCH

The LORD is good; His mercy is everlasting, and His truth endures to all generations.

PSALM 100:5

Teach us
to escape
the worries
of this world,
to live and
rest in You.

HARRIET CROSBY

God is love, and he who abides in love
abides in God, and God in him.

1 JOHN 4:16

*Never question God's great love,
for it is as unchangeable
a part of God
as is His holiness.*

BILLY GRAHAM

Lyn Babbitt

Delight yourself also in the LORD,
and He shall give you the desires of your heart.

PSALM 37:4

God has designed us for
happiness. He has created us
for peace and joy.

CATHERINE MARSHALL

Whoever desires to save his life will lose it,
but whoever loses his life for My sake will find it.

MATTHEW 16:25

Let our life
be one of
self-sacrifice,
finding our
highest joy
in blessing others.

ANDREW MURRAY

The LORD is good to all,
and His tender mercies
are over all His works.

PSALM 145:9

Whatever happens to me
each day is my daily bread,
provided I do not refuse
to take it from God's hand,
and to feed upon it.

FRANÇOIS FENELON

It is God who works in you both to will
and to do for His good pleasure.

PHILIPPIANS 2:13

When we put our lives
into God's hands and
ask Him to direct us,
amazing results will follow.

CATHERINE MARSHALL

Let the hearts of those *rejoice who seek the LORD.*
PSALM 105:3

Finding joy means first of all finding Jesus.

JILL BRISCOE

He has made everything beautiful in its time.

ECCLESIASTES 3:11

*The Lord's goodness
is the source
of all our joy.*

C. H. SPURGEON

Ointment and perfume delight the heart,
and the sweetness of a . . . friend gives
delight by hearty counsel.

PROVERBS 27:9

*The best thing
one woman
can give to another
is the warm hand
of understanding.*

BARBARA JENKINS

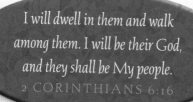

I will dwell in them and walk among them. I will be their God, and they shall be My people.

2 CORINTHIANS 6:16

Keep close to God, and then you need fear nothing.

JOSEPH ELIOT

Gwendolyn Babbitt © 1991

Blessed are those who keep His testimonies,
who seek Him with the whole heart.

PSALM 119:2

Obey God one step at a time,
then the next step
will come into view.

CATHERINE MARSHALL

If you walk in My statutes and keep My commandments, ... I will give peace in the land.

LEVITICUS 26:3–6

A wise companion is half the journey.

RUSSIAN PROVERB

He who has begun a good work in you
will complete it until the day of Jesus Christ.

PHILIPPIANS 1:6

*He made you and therefore
He understands you and knows
how to manage you. You must
trust Him to do it.*

HANNAH WHITALL SMITH

Wisdom is better than rubies, and all the things one may desire cannot be compared with her.

PROVERBS 8:11

It is easier to get older than wiser.

BARBARA JOHNSON

My times
are in Thy hand,
O Lord!
And, surely,
that is the best.

ROBERT LEIGHTON

He will not allow your foot to be moved;
He who keeps you will not slumber.

PSALM 121:3

It is not good to eat much honey;
so to seek one's own glory is not glory.

PROVERBS 25:27

If you are the best,
don't tell others—
that's what
friends are for.

VERONIQUE VIENNE

lya Babbitt

I am the vine, you are the branches.
He who abides in me, and I in him,
bears much fruit.

JOHN 15:5

*The will
of God
is the expression
of His love.*

WARREN W. WIERSBE

Commit your way to the LORD,
trust also in Him, and He shall bring it to pass.

PSALM 37:5

Trust in God changes
the way you live.

REBBE MENACHEM SCHNEERSON

My God shall supply all your need according to His riches in glory by Christ Jesus.

PHILIPPIANS 4:19

My business is to think about God. It is for God to think about me.

SIMONE WEIL

If you keep My commandments,
you will abide in My love.

JOHN 15:10

We are most useful to God
when poured free of self
and full of Christ.

BETH MOORE

In the night His song shall be with me—
a prayer to the God of my life.

PSALM 42:8

*God Himself is the answer
to all questions.*

JONI EARECKSON TADA

The LORD is good to all,
and His tender mercies are over all His works.

PSALM 145:9

We take Him as our Master,
and He takes us as His friends.

HUGH BLACK

God is greater than our heart, and knows all things.

1 JOHN 3:20

God is always far more willing
to give us good things than we
are anxious to have them.

CATHERINE MARSHALL

If two of you agree on earth concerning anything that they ask, it will be done for them by My Father in heaven.

MATTHEW 18:19

Let us pray for each other, for this is the best way to love one another.

MOTHER TERESA

You will keep him in perfect peace whose mind
is stayed on You, because he trusts in You.

ISAIAH 26:3

Teach us to escape
the worries
of this world,
to live and
rest in you.

HARRIET CROSBY

The LORD is
my strength and song,
and He has become
my salvation.

EXODUS 15:2

It's not so much what
happens to you; it's how you
handle the happenings.

BARBARA JOHNSON

The Father Himself loves you,
because you have loved Me.

JOHN 16:27

*God is not only
all-powerful. He is
perfect in goodness.*

RAVI ZACHARIAS

Pleasant words are like a honeycomb,
sweetness to the soul and health to the bones.

PROVERBS 16:24

*Friends remind us
we are part of something
greater than ourselves.*

BARBARA JENKINS

You, O LORD, will bless the righteous;
with favor You will surround him as with a shield.

PSALM 5:12

All of life is a gift,
and God has given
it for joy.

TERRY LINDVALL

In the fear of the LORD there is strong confidence,
and His children will have a place of refuge.

PROVERBS 14:26

Lord, we are rivers,
running to Thy sea,
our waves and ripples
all derived from Thee:
A nothing we should have,
a nothing be, except for Thee.

CHRISTINA ROSSETTI

Be tenderhearted, ... that you
may inherit a blessing.

1 PETER 3:8-9

*The tongue is the
ambassador of
the heart.*

JOHN LYLY

I will strengthen them in the LORD,
and they shall walk up and down in His name.

ZECHARIAH 10:12

*Prayer draws down the great
God into the little heart.*

MECHTHILDE OF MAGDEBURG

The work of righteousness will be peace,
and the effect of righteousness, quietness
and assurance forever.

ISAIAH 32:17

*The peace of God
follows the songs of faith.*

JAN CARLBERG

The Son of God has come
and has given us an understanding,
that we may know Him who is true.

1 JOHN 5:20

Faith is a gift, but for very
few is it a gift given without
any demand for equal time
devoted to its cultivation.

FLANNERY O'CONNOR

I praise Thee
while my days go on;
I love Thee while
my days go on;
I thank Thee
while my days go on.

ELIZABETH BARRETT BROWNING

He will teach us His ways,
and we shall walk in His paths.

MICAH 4:2

How precious little deeds
of love and sympathy are;
How strong to bless,
how easy to perform,
How comfortable to recall.

LOUISA MAY ALCOTT

God bless you
and keep you
dear friend.